MY BODY, YOUR BODY

MICK MANNING AND BRITA GRANSTRÖM

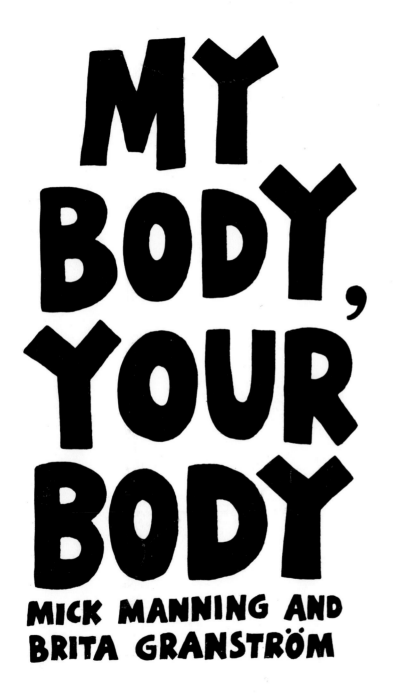

W
FRANKLIN WATTS
A Division of Grolier Publishing
NEW YORK • LONDON • HONG KONG • SYDNEY
DANBURY, CONNECTICUT

Look in a mirror!

What color are your eyes? Perhaps they are brown, blue, green, or grey. Eyes let us see the world we live in.

Close your eyes and imagine what it feels like not to see anything at all!

A giant squid's eye is as big as a football!

Eagles' eyes are the same size as human eyes, but they are as powerful as a pair of binoculars.

Tarsiers, like bush babies and cats, have special eyes to see in the dark.

Listen!

Your world is full of noise. Your ears hear thousands of different sounds every day.

Your ear flap helps collect sounds and protects your "earhole"!

African elephants have ear flaps as big as bedsheets! They flap them to keep cool and spread them wide when they are angry...

Bats use their big ears to listen for flying insects...

Crickets have their ears in their knees!

Take a big sniff!

Your nose is a smelling machine!
You can smell about ten thousand
different smells with it.

A dog's sense of smell is as much as a million times better than ours!

A housefly can smell meat from the other side of town!

An elephant's trunk is both its nose and its top lip! It can suck up water and even be an extra arm.

A star-nosed mole has tentacles on its nose for feeling as well as smelling!

A shark can smell food from far away!

Stick out your tongue!

Your tongue can tell the difference between sour, sweet, salty, and bitter tastes. It also helps to move food around your mouth and swallow it.

A toad only takes a split second to flick out its tongue and lasso an insect.

If you had a tongue as long as an anteater's it would stretch down to your knees!

Giraffes' black tongues are long enough to clean their ears with!

Shout out loud!

aaaaaaah!

oooo?!

Feel the air make your voicebox vibrate like the strings of a musical instrument. With the help of your lips and tongue you can make words and sing.

Hell !!

Hell .

Hell !!

Oooo

A blue whale's voice is the loudest voice on Earth.

ah!

Parrots can copy human words!

Croak!

Some frogs call by filling a special throat bag with air!

Explore your teeth!

Feel them with your tongue — some are sharp for biting food and some are bumpy for chewing.

You will have 32 teeth in your mouth by the time you are a grown-up.

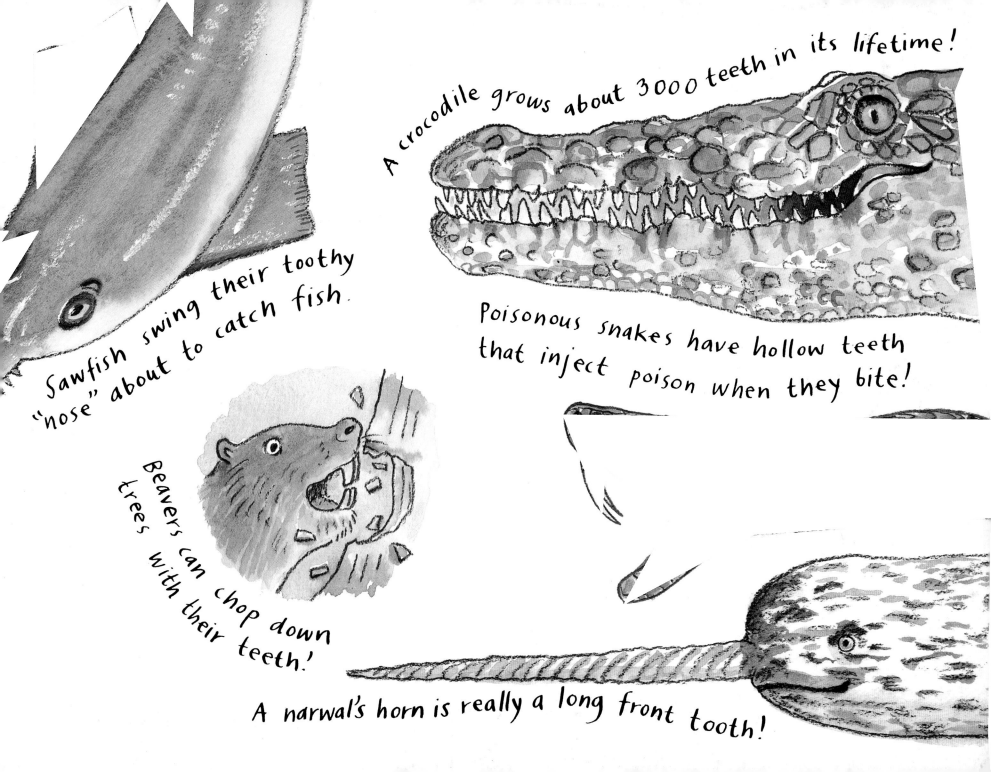

A crocodile grows about 3000 teeth in its lifetime!

Sawfish swing their toothy "nose" about to catch fish.

Poisonous snakes have hollow teeth that inject poison when they bite!

Beavers can chop down trees with their teeth!

A narwal's horn is really a long front tooth!

Stroke your head!

You have hundreds of thousands of hairs just on your head alone.

A male lion has a mass of beautiful shaggy hair called a mane.

In the freezing arctic, musk oxen need thick fur to stay warm!

Tenrecs have spiny hairs for protection.

Squeeze your arm!

Feel your muscles!
You have 650 muscles in your body. They help you move about and lift things.
Guess what your biggest muscle is.

Your biggest muscle is your behind!

Salmon are so strong they can swim up waterfalls!

Young orangutans are strong enough to swing among the treetops all day!

Ants can carry up to fifty times their own weight in one trip!

17

Tickle your ribs!

They are a bony cage for all the soft insides in your chest. All the bones that hold you together are called a skeleton.

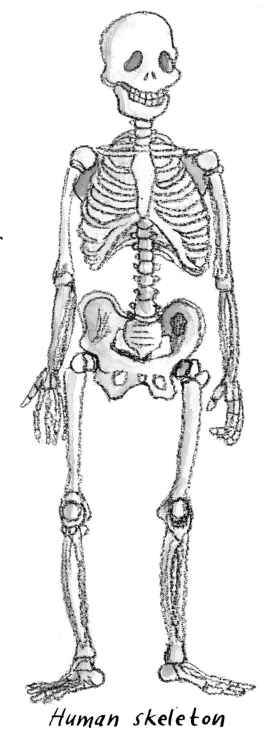

Human skeleton

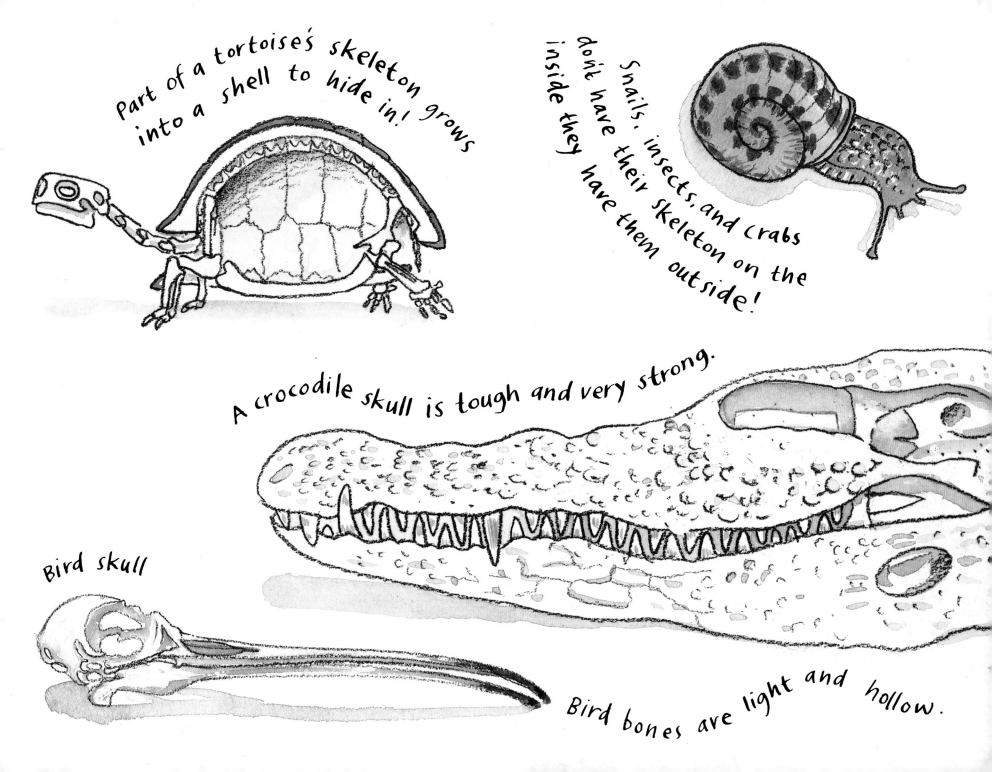

Part of a tortoise's skeleton grows into a shell to hide in!

Snails, insects, and crabs don't have their skeleton on the inside they have them outside!

A crocodile skull is tough and very strong.

Bird skull

Bird bones are light and hollow.

Jump around!

Strong bones and muscles in your legs help you to walk, hop, skip, and jump.

Roadrunners' leg muscles help them to run very fast to catch snakes and lizards.

Cheetahs are the fastest land animals on Earth.

A kangaroo rat can hop the length of a bus every second!

A flea can jump so high it would be like you hopping over a skyscraper!

Pinch your skin!

It feels soft, but it is a tough head-to-toe covering to protect you from the heat, dirt, and dust of the outside world.

If you hurt yourself your skin makes a scab of dried blood to protect itself while new skin grows underneath...

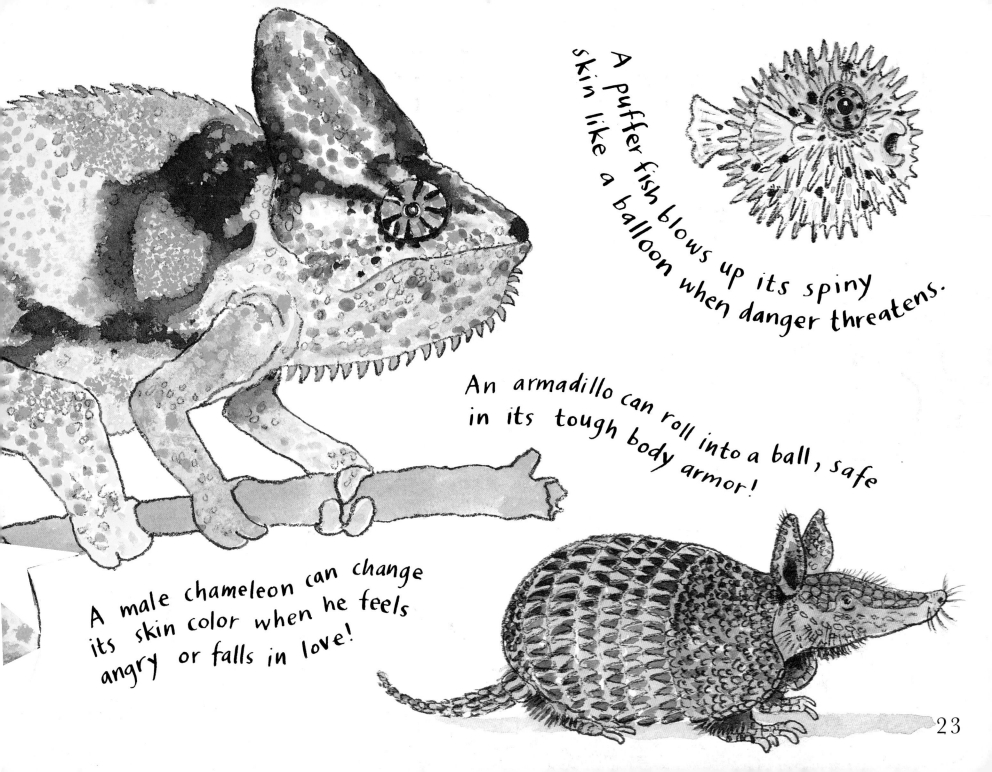

A puffer fish blows up its spiny skin like a balloon when danger threatens.

An armadillo can roll into a ball, safe in its tough body armor!

A male chameleon can change its skin color when he feels angry or falls in love!

23

Think about something...

Think about happy things ...
that's your brain working!
Think about yesterday... that's
your brain remembering!
Your brain makes you think,
see, talk, feel, laugh, and cry.
It tells you when you are hungry
and when to go to the bathroom.

Even when you are asleep your brain is working, sorting out your day's thoughts - that's what your dreams are! Dogs dream just like we do...

Gorillas have brains very like humans...

Now, let's do it one more time...

Look in the mirror!   Listen!   Take a big sniff!

Stick out your tongue!   Shout out loud!   Explore your teeth!

Stroke your head!

Squeeze your arm!

Tickle your ribs!

Jump around!

Pinch your skin!

Think about something!

All animals live their own special lives with their own special bodies — including us!

So, that's my body and that's your body!

Helpful words

Bitter like the taste of lemon or orange peel (see page 8).

Eagles and hawks have very powerful eyes so they can see the small animals they hunt from far above the ground (see page 3).

Skeleton is the framework of bones that holds you together. You'd be as floppy as a bean bag without it (see page 18).

Skull is the sort of bony helmet which protects your brain (see page 19).

Sweet like the taste of sugar (see page 8).

Bitter like the taste of banana skin or orange peel (see page 8).

Tenrecs small shrew-like animals (see page 15).

Skeleton is the framework of bones that holds you together.
You'd be as floppy as a bean bag without it (see page 18).

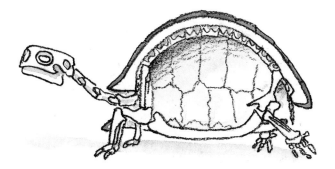

©1997 Franklin Watts
First American Edition 1997 by
Franklin Watts, A Division of Grolier Publishing
90 Sherman Turnpike, Danbury, CT 06816
Text and illustrations © Mick Manning and Brita Granström 1996
Series editor: Paula Borton
Printed in Singapore

Library of Congress Cataloging-in-Publication data

Manning, Mick.
    My body, your body / Mick Manning and Brita Granström.
        p. cm. - - (Wonderwise)
Summary : Compares and contrasts various parts of the human anatomy
with those of animals and concludes that all bodies are different
and special.
        ISBN 0-531-14486-0 (hardcover). - - ISBN 0-531-15324-X (pbk.)
1. Body, Human--Juvenile literature.   2. Anatomy, Comparative-
-Juvenile literature.   [1. Body, Human. 2. Anatomy, Comparative.]
I. Granström, Brita.   II. Title. III. Series.
QM27. M36 1997
611 --dc21   97-10727
                                                             CIP
                                                             AC